EVERY MORNING A FOOT IS LOOKING FOR MY NECK

Other titles from Central Square Press

A HARD SUMMATION by Afaa Michael Weaver (2014)

CRACKED CALABASH by Lisa Pegram (2015)

THE NEXT VERSE POETS MIXTAPE - VOLUME ONE: THE 4 x 4 by Melanie Henderson, Fred Joiner, Lisa Pegram, Enzo Silon Surin (2016)

FEAR OF DOGS & OTHER ANIMALS by Shauna M. Morgan (2016)

A LETTER OF RESIGNATION: AN AMERICAN LIBRETTO (2017) by Enzo Silon Surin

LETTERS FROM CONGO by Danielle Legros Georges (2017)

DEPARTURE by Samuel Miranda (2017)

UNDERWORLDS by Patrick Sylvain (2018)

A HOUSE IN ITS HUNGER by Jennifer Steele (2018)

EVERY MORNING A FOOT IS LOOKING FOR MY NECK

poems

Bonita Lee Penn

CENTRAL SQUARE PRESS

Copyright © 2019 by Bonita Lee Penn.

All rights reserved. No part of this book may be used or reproduced in any manner whatsoever without written permission from the publisher, except in the case of brief quotations embodied in critical articles or reviews.

All inquiries and permissions requests should be addressed to the Publisher:

Central Square Press
Lynn, Massachusetts

publisher@centralsquarepress.com
www.centralsquarepress.com

Printed in the United States of America
First Edition

ISBN-13: 978-1-941604-09-0

ISBN-10: 1-941604-09-9

Thank you to the editors of the following publication in which some of these poems, or versions of them, first appeared:

Joint Literary Magazine, Hot Metal Bridge Journal, Giantology (HAGL), Solstice Literary Magazine, and especially The Massachusetts Review and WSQ for being among the first.

Cover art: "The Daughter–Rhudiannjah" by Brianna McCarthy

Book design: Enzo Silon Surin

for Joseph and Marlene Lee
who are my roots

and for Winter, Simone and Venezuela
who are my flowers.

CONTENTS

Introduction by Enzo Silon Surin	IX
They — will, come for us	3
Rosary Prayers	5
In Our Room by Ourselves	7
Nights Tinker Bell Wore Combat Boots	9
Another Weight Loss Story	11
When the Walls Close In	13
Death Study	15
Secret Elegance of Flight When We Soar	
Furious Winds	17
every morning a foot is looking for my neck	18
MISSISSIPPI	19
May's Obituary in 2016	21
Being a Single Black Woman, on a Moonlit	
Night When Lightening Rides Thunder Bareback	23
Gratitude	24
Notes	25
About the Author	27

INTRODUCTION

Sometimes the cadence of our experiences cannot be expressed with traditional language and one must find a pace and rhythm that bellows what the mouth cannot. Bonita Lee Penn has done so with her chapbook of poems, EVERY MORNING A FOOT IS LOOKING FOR MY NECK. Whether it is the thumping of a heart or a black body hitting the ground prematurely, her words elegize the cries of those who have left us in a violent frenzy and bring to light an all too familiar ache with wit, fire and a haunting truth.

In this striking debut collection, Penn is unrelenting in the pushback against a world that tries to force us "to press our-/ selves into the recesses, into shadows / of our skin. to lay low, to be silent, to / shrink. disappear." These are vibrant and brilliant poems.

—Enzo Silon Surin,
Founding Editor & Publisher

every morning a foot is
looking for my neck

They — will, come for us

after streets are cleaned of chalked frames,
as the skin dries in mid-day sun, its flesh burns through
asphalt, smells of rubber and fresh polk that waits to die
on tongues that whisper round corners, "they coming"

us,
- multi-hued bangles, of green, of glass, a consummation, her suhaag.
- polychrome textiles, hand-dyed polished bazin, colours, alluring.
- fabrics bangs challenged skirts, universal quest to control women's bodies.

our blood—paint on crowded living room walls,
our flesh—food plastered on yesterday's meals,
our songs—menus of stolen this and that,

our worth—coupons for empty houses stamped
and bare refrigerators, sticky patched linoleum
that ever after returns to that place of suffice rage,
drank like red kool aide in bandaged bottles

our voices—shroud in pulp wrapped twisted twine,
that refuses to endure, change.

"for us"
packed in New Delhi public buses, hustle the dust of
India's own strange fruited trees—bloom feministic scent
and its split-tail petals hums *sangeet*, as they hang from trees

"they coming for us"
vegetated myths hack through the heart of darkness' fertility,
as inverted hymens of herded schoolgirls polish machetes,
and Congolese drums talk of butchery's blood, diminishes
Mandela's freedom walk, unravels peace, buried in cultures
"they coming, for us"
— now.

Rosary Prayers

Dyin ain't pretty. Sure
ain't streets dyin. Pretty
ain't it. In multi-plex castles
Black women die, kneelin,
prayin for enemies,
rockin dead weight.

Praisin hard life.
Lives lonely, lives.

Many teared eyes, full drops.
Rough hands ain't neva been
pretty.

Ironin. Washin. Cookin.
Spread table,
legs, okra, hominy, mush. Vines, faces
twisted. Eyes redd up.
Woulda.
Coulda.
If lovin a Black man is a full stomach: malnutrition stalks
Black women. If *basics*, held jobs.
Mothers, so many, on knees.
Arched hearts. Spines bent,
heavy vessels.
Laid down.

Love
no more.
Love unknown songs of mothers.
Restricted to marches. For mothered sons. Not plenty lovin.
Black women lovin canned tight. Untouched on sale shelves.
Hardened, faded. Run away lovin.
Caught in snared lives.
Chalk bags stuffed. Muffled screams. Knuckled heads, fists, faced palms out. A wasted submission.
Lovin dyin ain't pretty.
Black women's
hearts.

In our Room by Ourselves

> *"However, in the process of keeping up the appearance of strength, Black women's bodies become repositories for the thoughts, feelings and realities that contradict the one-dimensional view of them as unflaggingly capable and ever resilient."* —"A Half-Told Tale of Black Womanhood"

we cry. monsoons erode our bodies.
like earth's quakes of mud slides
this physical nothingness trembles to
cries echo cross continents and oceans.
the gravel beneath our bare feet tremors.

the ground opens—a sink-hole. a flush of
soil and we, disappear. we are buried with
mouths exposed. a waxen lid the earth
entombs our bodies. our tears flood rivers.
seal our eyes. light is not required to see

paths of stars, electric dream patterns. and,
we sleep as the earth constrains our bodies.
the pressure snaps bones, tendons spring
free. our skin explodes and we, are hurled
in every, each direction. we are compost,

flung across the universe. our veins stretch
the longitudes and latitudes of victories. yet,
we bleed. from our eyes. our noses. our ears.
soles of our feet. palms of our hands. we bleed
out from our brains. our mouths stitched shut.

our vaginas preserved as pickled yams. yet we sing. what space, inside our room, rejoices in chants? we are the earth's core. buried and torn apart, thrown as treasure in a scavenger hunt, to be found. we wait. to be found. and we wait.

Nights Tinker Bell Wore Combat Boots

Listen children you too, shall hear tales of Peter
& feisty Tinker Bell
who was always up in the brotha's ear.

Once, upon a midnight blue—naw bro, ebony night.
Peter exchanged his sissified dress, signifying tights
  for a restoration of
                      black power independence
                      ass-stomping brogan boots.

Fly way cool
              way fly cool

militant jacket — black leather, beret left cocked
tightrope his large bush.

Hoisted—loaded shotgun, stag-o-lee lean against right
ear- knocked Tinker hard, to the ground. Paa-Pow!

She leaped, stomped power dust from her combat boots
re-shape proudly her 10-point fro, screamed:
    death to racist pigs
high-fived her fellow fro'd, fisted sista Elaine Brown:
    who promptly cleared the shit up.

Shh   listen closely to urban tales of revolutionists, sang
in ghetto patois, un-translated by COINTELPRO's
bourgeois beds

Once, upon a beautiful mother-fuckin' ebony night, Peter & Tinker took flight under cover of darkness, mission- to release incarcerated militants from sleep, yo!

You still. . .

Another Weight Loss Story

her journey through weight loss
sounds something like
gun shots
desolation
        that endless wind as it echoes through
        subway systems
a disease walking, a deceased mass
a body abandoned, dumped by the
curb
        burial forgotten
a body all decorated
        and no body to dance with

her journey through weight loss
a morning dose of PTSD shake up
a reversal detox
a thickness that fills her with
bile, that lays its stench on her tongue
        like tar

add up negative points
minus
        mental health services/screenings
add up negative points
        poor depressed neighborhood

a depression that catches the bus with her
wants to touch her hair

identity depressed
    her only choice is a therapist who
    does not look like her
who only knows her through reality shows
and textbooks based on their false perceptions
based on lies, half-truths

    the ink blot they show her
sounds like gun fire, sounds like screams
    the ink blot they show her
a spreadsheet that illustrates
    what kind of gun makes that noise
that measures
    the distance from her house, to gun shots,
    from her house, to the playgrounds
    to the corner stores, to the bus stops,
    to the subway platforms

    the ink blot they show her
is a calculation of how many children are
in the area of the gun shots, the probability
if her child(ren) are in the vicinity

    the ink blot they show her
is a yellow barrier taped around the city swings,
the sliding boards, the free throw line on the cement
basketball court, horse "x's" are the bodies.

When the Walls Close In

when women were the ones to
dress the dead
the dead drugged out from rivers
the dead littered in street gutters
uncovered for hours until the yellow tape
withered

bodies dead, disrespected, that disgusting
taste left in mouths
that sets up house in their minds

countless screams, and they cry
and they cry
and they cry
and they cry
and they
cry

and they walk from one wall to next
with their fists tight
and they walk from the window to
the wall
and people sit outside their doors
and they cry
and they curse, cause
they cry, and
they don't know what else to do

the trauma confesses itself in their minds
a trigger reaction to the release of the triggers
the clicks on repeat
like the moon disappears in the day
but it is- but it is still there

the trauma reflects in windows
and mirrors, and words
found written on yellow wallpaper

Death Study

they spit on [y]our children
- call them little niggers

they scream at [y]our children
- cut off their natural locs

and yell at [y]our children
- defame their natural language

then they AD
HD [y]our children

arrest [y]our children
then [y]our children hang themselves
in locked jail cells

and [y]our children stop breathing

and [y]our children are shot in the back

and they are shot in the face

and they are asked for driver's license
registration and they are shot

and they are asked to get out the car

why do [y]our children commit self-suicide

why is [y]our happiness threatening

why is [y]our being alive threatening

and all the
drummingclapbacks
will not protect [y]our children

and [y]our children march to protest
and they are tear gassed

and [y]our children protest and march
and [y]our children are tear gassed

why are [y]our children bully clubbed
tasered, and arrested

it all begins again

yet, you sit back, and wonder
why do [y]our children continue to die

Secret Elegance of Flight When We Soar Furious Winds

'cause we be allowed to be fine like this
eyelashes glued and flutter like wings
        of an albatross
cool our bodies as we walk the walk in the 24/7
        summer heat that is our blood.

we walk in formation in sky blue ripped, shredded skinny jeans
        and our titties pressed tight as nipples sing cause we
            pretty and pretty sings.

we are baddd, this, what we got from the
        Carolyn Rodgers
        Sonia Sanchez
            baddd m.f. truth-saying sisters.

that symbolic glitter of our magic, that does not quietly fall
        to the ground, we, sound more like hydrogen bombs.

'cause we loud   and we pretty.

and our eyelashes flutters like death's ashes blows in the wind.
        we here, and everywhere, and here where we be.

every morning a foot is looking for my neck

roll porcupine tight
squeeze in between tight
out the way spaces.

disappear.

told us to carry the burdens:
nasty, dirty, big booty, black
and racist, big-hips and bitter
feminist, revolutionist pissed
poet. shadow of an evil-eyed
animal. not woman enough
to be loved, a wife, never a
mother. one of those uppity,
mixed-up bitches, one of them
too educated m.f.'ers. ignore her.
screw her. throw her away.

shove her in a dark corner. evict
her from her own box. bury her.
silence her. erase her humanity in
stained exotic porno-post cards,
dressed in veils, habib, or bananas.

the world yells and tells us to be
a chameleon. to blend, to press our-
selves into the recesses, into shadows
of our skin. to lay low, to be silent, to
shrink. disappear.

MISSISSIPPI

bloated bodies   those floaters
        mississippi's   mud pies.

pall bearers foot prints   blood baptized
after the neck snaps
after the bough breaks
after the nigger chased   is won.

bodies hidden under floor boards
underground, in root cellars
        who will sing for bodies found *in the river?*

mothers want to know- if bodies be drunk with
bullets- if a leg be missing- if the penis be shoved
in mouths—

cause, it is, the black women who clean the bodies
try to make them honorable for burial.

twine tight round necks
stomachs slashed opened   filled with river rocks
and the river   rocks
        take me to the river   take me to the river
        take me to —

the dragged bodies–are–yanked to river's edge, found by
the light of the silver moon–shine   had   nothing to do
with the howls heard,

howls pour out of darkness
        a shot glass filled with dark liquor
        guzzled down, burns   fleshy throats.

the flesh filled with bullets, the hog-tied flesh
flesh dragged up, from the river's gut.

May's Obituary in 2016

> *"The greatest purveyor of violence on earth*
> *is my own government."* -Martin Luther King, Jr.

May Obituary lists the names of Black bodies
Hollowed be their names. Numerous names. Naming names.
Hand-me down names. No order names. No reason names.
>Michelle, Bruce, Talif, Deborah.
>Korryn, Norman, Joyce, India.
>Kisha, Mark, Lavar, Shalah.
>Maneia, Terrell, Kajuan, Antwon.

What names do we give our dead?
>Beloved, proud, devoted.

In the name of the fathers, the names of our brothers,
In the name of our sisters, the names the mothers.

Of the names burnt on their backs
>Nigger. Criminal. Person of Interest/
>Suspect/Person of Interest. Terrorist.

Black bodies left dead in the streets of
>Cleveland, Tampa, Brooklyn, Oakland.
>Dallas, Ferguson, Las Vegas, Morgantown.
>Rock Island, Tucson, Jacksonville, Houston.

Most livable cities paved with dead Black bodies

Scent of decayed bodies, like those of long summer days.
        Landover, Baltimore, Pittsburgh, Eastaboga.
        Indianapolis, Lansing, Miami, Flagstaff.

The names transportable, dead Black bodies found in every city.
        Ollie Brooks. Jabril Robinson. Jessica Williams.
        Arthur Williams, Jr. Matthew Tucker. Osee Calix.
        Dennis Hudson. Jabril Robinson. Deresha Armstrong.

Age at time of death
a combination of dice rolls
snake eyes. Game over. Black bodies never
too young or old.
To be dead. Die.
        12, 18, 56, 23, 33, *how old they is?*
        70, 38, 53, 32, 25, *bullets don't see age.*
        58, 59, 19, 21, 43, *they do see skin color.*

May of 2016 bloomed more than flowers, it buried Black bodies.
May 30th, May 29th, May 28th, May 27th, *and again*
May 26th, May 24th, May 23rd, May 22nd, *then again*
May 20th, May 19th, May 18th, *and on*
May 16th, May 13th, May 11th, *and again on*
May 10th, May 9th, May 8th, May 7th, *again*
May 5th, May 4th, May 1st, *killed* . . .

Being a Single Black Woman, on a Moonlit Night When Lightening Rides Thunder Bareback

is all that is seen / piano keys dance / click and clack / kick, slides cross empty palms / snap of heels on concrete stairs / ledge unsteady as hot wind hurries through a field / cane field / flames chase / sweet douse of tears that stopped crawling out lids / wet love potions / mixture of red clay / mother's land soil that sleeps on forest floors / selected winds that surf tall field grass and hollers between cotton barbs / drops of sun rays burnt through levees / scrapple of vodou watchwords / drowns the battlegrounds drawn in the silence of black men. / deep- red bone legit ligaments disconnect / but inner connectivity to what ails lonely thighs / tightly loose and ready to jump / how wide. / rainbow's toss sprinkles to douse her flames / speaks of nefertari and sheba's yoruba's second cousin who spoke ibo / and dressed in mudcloth / and carried a nguni shield but spoke xhosa / this black male smoke screen all over the place / as her emotions / as she fidgets in her emptiness / in thoughts of a man who may speak ibo / xhosa / blackened english / and who holds his head high for the love of clean water and black women / whose songs are wild hurricanes.

GRATITUDE

"I am a Black Woman poet and I [proudly] sound like one," thank you Lucille Clifton and to all Black women whose words I have sharpened my teeth.

Much appreciation to those who invited me to share my poetry at their readings, and to those in attendance who were the first to hear many of these poems read out loud.

Thank you to Solstice Literary Magazine who named "When Lightening Rides Thunder Bareback" the Editor's Pick for their 2018 Summer issue.

NOTES

1. The epigraph in "In our Room by Ourselves" is from Tamara Beauboeuf-Lafontant's book, <u>Behind the Mask of the Strong Black Woman: Voice & the Embodiment of a Costly Performance</u> (Temple University Press, 2009).

2. "Nights Tinker Bell Wore Combat Boots" reflects on the United States Federal Bureau of Investigation's (FBI) COunter INTELligence PROgram (1956–1971). The program used, at times, illegal surveillance and infiltration to discredit/disrupt Black organizations. Such as the Black Panther Party, Martin Luther King, Jr., Malcolm X, Nation of Islam and Black Lives Matter.

3. Rosary Prayers: "*basics*" – Basic is slang for a Black woman/man who works low paying jobs (those positions always offered to unskilled Blacks) and they are happy just working. Won't apply themselves to move upwards in the organization. They are happy being basic.

4. "When the Walls Close In" references Charlotte Perkins Gilman's short story <u>The Yellow Wallpaper</u> (published 1892). It illustrates the attitudes of a patriarchal society's views towards mental/physical health of women, in addition to its oppression, that discourages women from being creative as it was viewed as a sign of defiance.

5. Inspiration for "M I S S I S S I P P I" comes from the poetic/musical piece "Mr. Sippy" written and performed by Heroes are Gang Leaders.

6. The data used in "May's Obituary in 2016" was gathered from: "Police Shootings 2016 Database." The Washington Post, WP Company, www.washingtonpost.com/graphics/national/police-shootings-2016/.

7. The title poem "every morning a foot is looking for my neck" signifies a condition of humiliation; for someone in a position of power to have control over another or to have another person in a vulnerable position.

ABOUT THE AUTHOR

BONITA LEE PENN is a Pittsburgh poet, editor, curator and author of the chapbook, **EVERY MORNING A FOOT IS LOOKING FOR MY NECK** (Central Square Press). Her work has appeared in numerous publications and her poem "When Lightning Rides Thunder Bareback" was the Solstice Editors' Pick for the 2018 summer issue of *Solstice: A Magazine of Diverse Voices*. She is Managing Editor of the Soul Pitt Quarterly Magazine and co-curator of "Common Threads: Faith, Activism, and the Art of Healing," a Pittsburgh-based art exhibit that examines the political, social, cultural, and aesthetic priorities of women of varying faith traditions.

www.ingramcontent.com/pod-product-compliance
Lightning Source LLC
Chambersburg PA
CBHW052210110526
44591CB00012B/2150